PAIDEIA MONOGRAPHS

POINT
COUNTER
POINT

H. EVAN
RUNNER

www.paideiapress.ca
www.reformationaldl.org

Point Counter Point

This English monograph edition is a publication of Paideia Press (3248 Twenty First St., Jordan Station, Ontario, Canada L0R 1S0). Copyright ©2020 by Paideia Press. All rights reserved.

Except for brief quotations in critical publications or reviews, no part of this book may be reproduced in any manner without prior written permission from Paideia Press at the address above.

Unless otherwise indicated, Scripture quotations are from the ESV® Bible (The Holy Bible, English Standard Version®). Copyright © 2001 by Crossway, a publishing ministry of Good News Publishers. Used by permission. All rights reserved.

Paideia Monograph Series Editor: Steven R. Martins

Book Design by: Steven R. Martins

ISBN 978-0-88815-268-8

Printed in the United States of America

Contents

Opening Words	5
The Complexity of our Time	8
Our Calling	19
Point Counter Point	39
Closing Words	53
About the Author	55

POINT
COUNTER
POINT

Opening Words

WHAT A DAY THIS IS TO BE ALIVE! How full of consequence for the life of future generations! How crucial for all the English-speaking nations, and even, as we hope, for far beyond! We come today introducing into the life of this nation and of this continent a new institution (the ICS). More weighty is the fact that for the English-speaking world it is even a new, an unheard of kind of institution. The emergence of this new thing means that a new concentration of forces is taking shape. It signifies a re-organization of our human and material resources to accomplish a task not yet undertaken. There is a re-alignment with the avowed purpose of carrying out the Christian Mission in higher education in a manner and to a degree never hitherto attempted on our continent. This is a radical Christian proposal for radical times. Karl Marx is justly celebrated for his remark: "To be radical is to go to the root of the question. Now the root of mankind is man." Since Marx, all of us are being driven more and more to the root of the question. Our attention is now going to have to be centered upon things which previously, if they have been given any consideration at all, have been considered only very incidentally and peripherally. This charting of a new course is what clearly marks the event we are witnessing here today as an historic event. Events of this kind are to be experienced only very infrequently. Who of us, for example, were present when the Free Reformed University of Amsterdam was opened in the Netherlands on October 19-20, 1880? Today, on this high-day of our own corporate life, what privilege it is to be alive and present in this chamber!

Such a rush of feelings and sentiments surges through us, now that we are come to this moment! Above all else, we are grateful to God on high, that He still, at a late hour in our history, graciously grants us the historical freedom to take this significant and decisive step that we are taking here this day.

There can be little doubt that our civilization is at one of its epoch-making turning points, as at the time of the Renaissance and the Reformation. There is now, as there was then, a remarkable quickening of the cultural impulse, an increased perception and sensitivity, a notable enlargement of experience. Yet there is also a critical difference. The intervening centuries have brought the Industrial Revolution and the development of political and social democracy. Huge systems of public education, if they have not evoked the truth that every many supposedly possessed within him, have at least brought an incredible accumulation of factual knowledge within the reach of every man. Today the masses have come on to the foreground. We encounter them everywhere. In just a single country, whether it be in the sphere of education or the arts or science, you have immediately to do with so many persons and so many centres of hustling activity. And then there are the many effect of computerization. Indeed, the current step-up in the tempo of cultural change, complicated by this state of affairs, is so unprecedented that someone has come up with the somewhat contrived term 'rapidation' to describe its uniqueness. Think only of the great scientific and technological advances of our time, the exploration of limitless sky, of depths of ocean, of the earth's poles, the changes in the ways we store information.

This aspect of our time, corresponding to the inventiveness, the intense cultivation of the arts and the expanding geographical horizons of the period of the Renaissance, should in itself be offering us hope for our expectations of the future. But it is frequently having a contrary effect. It leaves most of us gasping and terribly frustrated. Even the scientist who confines himself to only one subordinate area of his science finds it hopelessly impossible to keep pace with what is being thought and done within such a very restricted compass. In order to keep abreast of developments he feels the necessity of confining himself, but the confinement appears not to have a good effect on the quality of the scientific work that is done. Everything proves to be so intricately interrelated. Here you feel something of the *complexity* of our time.

The Complexity of our Time

The period of transition through which we are now passing is further complicated by a more ominous aspect, to which the complexity of which we have just spoken is not unrelated. Our time is a time of crisis, of fundamental crisis. Some years ago Prof. Pitirim Sorokin of Harvard University, one of the world's most eminent sociologists, wrote that:

> every important aspect of the life, organization and culture of the Western society is in extraordinary crisis…

Its body and mind are sick and there is hardly a spot on its body which is not sore, nor any nervous fiber which functions soundly.

In another place he says:

The crisis is also extraordinary in the sense that, like its predecessors, it is marked by an extraordinary explosion of wars, revolutions, anarchy, and bloodshed; by social, moral, economic, political, and intellectual chaos; by a resurgence of revolting cruelty and animality, and a temporary destruction of the great and small values of mankind; by misery and suffering on the part of millions – a convulsion far in excess of the chaos and disorganization of the ordinary crises.

Sorokin has certainly succeeded here in putting into a few words a great deal of what we have all been experiencing in our time. Yet there is something else that will have to be said. And that something else is not so much an addition as a modification in the perspective. We who bear the name of Christ must read history eschatologically: today we are nearer the End than we have ever been before.

It is interesting to note, for instance, in our Lord's great prophetic discourse, recorded in Luke 21, the comparison He makes between the time of the destruction of Jerusalem and the time of the Last Days. "The dreadful fate awaiting the people of Jerusalem" was to be so terrible that it is "held up as a clear foreshadowing of the Last Days and the Final Judgment." Still, there is a difference. Before the fall of Jerusalem there were to be signs in this place or that (v. 11); but "before the end of the age all creation and the whole of the human world – the *oikonmené* – (v. 25) will be plunged into dreadful commotions" (Geldenhnys). The events of the Last Days are distinctly characterized by their world-embracing character, all mankind being reduced to a state of trepidation through them. The figures used in speaking of the end-time, viz. "the roaring of the sea and the billows" are used in the Old Testament prophets as symbols of the violent overthrow of national systems and great empires.

It is just possible that not everyone who calls himself Christian will feel with us this sympathy. For in the history of Christianity, just as in the history of Judaism, there has been a long trend of withdrawal from the world and from the full life of society into secluded, private cultic communities that have scarcely deserved the name of church, communities that became more and more irrelevant and ineffectual as time went on. In these sequestered communities too there has been a strange preoccupation with the words of the Law, the words of Scripture, a narrow turning in of the *intellect* upon its many injunctions and prescriptions. Frequently there arose an arrogant confidence in theological niceties of our own systematic devising. Men retreated into fanciful dreams of allegory, numerology, dispensational-schematisms and the like. A rigoristic legalism and moralism set in. Spirituality was often sought in a kind of prayer and meditation that only drew men away from their life in the world.

This trend, which has extended over all the modern centuries, has only in recent decades begun here and there to be reversed. There is another breed of Christian emerging. The cause is re-discovery again in our time of the living and active and powerful Word of God.

Wherever in the past the Word or Law of God has been seen for what it is, there men have been torn away from their abstractions and brought back to fullness of life; they have been released from their enslavement to their narrow, introverted reasonings and experienced enlargement to a whole life of service of God according to His commandments in the world. When Bradwardine, Franciscan monk of the English pre-reformation, came under the influence of the Word of God as found in the later scriptural studies of Augustine, he re-discovered the scriptural notion of freedom from sin as the spontaneous service of God which God Himself had introduced into our spiritual death. Led by Augustine, Luther and Calvin too came to the Word of God. The immediate result is that we are torn from all the medieval metaphysical reasonings, and *religion*, man's relation to God, is in the foreground. Religion is now seen in its scriptural sense, not as a sort of subjectivistic introverted piety, but as the directedness of the heart or centre of our life to God Himself, which then further governs all the rest of our existence. As a result of the labour of these Reformers, Christendom was enabled with fresh courage to join battle with the forces of humanism. Not withdrawal from the world, but work and struggle in it, a contending with the spirits that are not of God and a firm standing in the Truth, which is the Word of God; – this was the consequence of the re-discovery of the Word of God in times past.

In the preceding century it was the discovery by Abraham Kuyper that the Reformed 'principle' was not an ecclesiastical or theological principle but a principle of *life* which led to the development of all sorts of Christian cultural action and to the founding of the Free University itself. Repeatedly Kuyper speaks of what had occurred in his experience as a 're-discovery' (*hereontdekking*).

Perhaps the clearest and quickest way to illustrate the difference between the kind of life that has so frequently in history characterized the Jewish and Christian communities and the LIFE that springs into being where men experience the Word of God for what it is, is to recall that very familiar story about the ark in 1 Samuel 4. The Israelites, bested in battle by the Philistines, are gathered in the camp, where the elders, in their experience of complete defeat, ask the unavoidable question, Why has the Lord put us to rout today before the Philistines? They then propose to bring the ark of the covenant of the Lord to the camp from Shiloh "that he may come among us and save us from the power of our enemies." You remember what happens. The ark is brought into the camp amidst mighty shouting. Puzzled by all the commotion, the Philistines are terrified when they hear, presumably from spies who have reconnoitered the enemy camp, what the cause of the shouting is. Screwing up their courage, however, they return to the battle, and this time inflict upon the Israelites more than seven times the previous number of casualties.

What has gone so terribly wrong? There can be no doubt that those elders of Israel knew to distinguish between a box and the God of the covenant. The difficulty is in their anthropocentric or egocentric or subjectivistic attitude. Israel has been living its life, such as it is, and fighting its wars as best it can, and then when unusual – I was going to say, supernatural – help is needed, thoughts turn to the ark and their God who dwells there. The ark, with the enthroned God, has shrunk in the experience of these Israelites to become something very much like a talisman that one manipulates according to one's desires and needs. *But all the while* the sovereign God, Creator of heaven and earth, Who had chosen Israel and gives Himself to that people, was there revealed, enthroned upon the cherubim. The ark symbolized the very presence of the living God in the midst of His people whom He had chosen to walk before Him according to His commandments and thereby to live. The Israelites had missed the fullness of life before the presence or Word of the living God and had narrowed their attention to the symbol. The symbol was on the way to becoming an idol. They killed the spirit with the letter. That is precisely the way it has so often been with us: the spirit of the Law and Word, which gives life, has been reduced to the killing letter; the Word of God has been experienced only as so many words.

How very different, by contrast, is David's bringing of the ark of Jerusalem. David is deeply conscious of the religious relation between God and the people. He is full of joy that the ark, which symbolizes the real meaning of what it is to be a Jew (to be of Israel), can now be brought into the capital city. As king, he advances before the presence of the Lord. David has not shrunk up to dissecting the symbol analytically or manipulating it. David lives in the full reality of the life-encompassing covenantal relation between the Lord and Israel. That covenant is the well-spring of all Israel's life, her hope, her growth, her strength – *in the world*.

In our generation we are once again experiencing a recovery of the Word of God in its integral meaning as the Beginning or Principle which gives direction and meaning to our whole life, to what we still, with the help of an old expression, speak of as our life – 'walk'. God's Word, we have come to understand, is not a collection of revealed logical propositions, conveying to us, after the natural sciences have rendered up to us a 'natural knowledge' of the 'natural world', some additional category of 'spiritual' knowledge about a hidden world of 'supernatural' entities. We have come to see that in His Word, God reveals *Himself* to us in the covenantal fellowship He has established with the people of His choice. The Word of God discloses and illumines this fellowship, which is at once the heart of all created reality and the central reality of our human existence. Such disclosure acts as the ordering principle of our lives. It pushes all other aspects of our lives out of this central place and makes of them so many distinct expressions of what is disclosed to be central.

Acknowledgment of this fundamental work of God's Self-revelation in our lives is what underlies the establishment of the Association for Reformed Scientific Studies. This recovery of the meaning of the Word of God, and it alone, is able to account for the determination that has marked our efforts to open this Institute. Here you will find the source and only ground of our confidence and our expectancy.

For though we shall undoubtedly be accused of being, we are certainly not reactionaries, attempting anachronistically to rehabilitate an old order that has had its day and proved its worth – or unworth.

Of course, if in Lenin's spirit all that is not perfectly in agreement with Lenin is to be called reactionary or counter-revolutionaries; for we are no Leninists. But from our present vantage-point where Leninism appears more and more to be itself counter-revolutionary in the sense of anti-progressive, we need not worry too much about the Leninist description of what constitutes reaction.

Those who find themselves agreeing with what Harvey Cox wrote in his widely read book *The Secular City* will also undoubtedly see us as just another example of contemporary reaction. Let me quote you a paragraph from the book:

The anachronistic posture of the church is nowhere more obvious than in the context of the university community. The church has made three attempts to come to terms with the university problem in America, all of which have been marked by a certain recidinism. The first was the establishment of its own colleges and universities. This of course is medievalism. The whole idea of a "Christian" college or university after the breaking apart of the medieval synthesis has little meaning. The term Christian is not one that can be used to refer to universities any more than to observatories or laboratories. No one of the so-called Christian colleges that now dot our Midwest is able to give a very plausible theological basis for retaining the equivocal phrase Christian college in the catalog. Granted that there may be excellent traditional, public-relations, or sentimental reasons for calling a college Christian, there are no theological reasons. The fact that it was founded by ministers, that it has a certain number of Christians on the faculty or in the student body, that chapel is required (or not required), or that it gets part of its bills paid by a denomination – none of these factors provides any grounds for labeling an institution with a word that the Bible applies only to followers of Christ, and then very sparingly. The idea of developing "Christian universities" in America was bankrupt even before it began.

If Cox, following the positivists' so-called Law of the Three Stages, has taken his stand in science, and from that (highly developed) position looks back down upon religion and metaphysics as earlier, less developed (and now anachronistic) forms of man's intellectual life, that is one thing. But then it should be pointed out, first, that to take a stand in science as the way to meaning is something more than to do science. It is to commit oneself in decision and faith. The act of commitment is not the same as the doing of science. In the second place, it ought also to be pointed out that to take one stand in science as the way to meaning is to commit oneself to an *un*authentic faith. For it can readily be shown that the very nature of the abstractions science deals with presupposes a more integral experience of the world, of things and of persons than science, in virtue of its own inner abstracting nature, can ever explain or even relate itself to. Analysis of the phenomenon we know as science discloses its relative and dependent character. It could certainly never be the way to meaning.

If, on the other hand, Cox is mainly reaching against those things in the history of Christianity which have been foreign to the divine Word-revelation – for instance, he speaks in the same section from which I read of "Western Christendom, based partly on the biblical

Gospel, partly on late Greek philosophy…" and says that the church "cherishes its timeworn rituals… preferably with ancestral costumes" and "limps along with a theology still not extricated from the metaphysical baggage to which it was firmly lashed during the opening centuries of the era" –; well, in that case, Cox will find us in strong agreement with him.

We are not just old theological reactionaries. We do not put our confidence in rituals and liturgies, in our denominational histories or our theological systems. That is not to deny the relative importance of any or all of these when they are themselves Scripture-directed. But our confidence is in the life-producing, life-sustaining, life-developing Word of our God.

Our Calling

We are averse to all escapes, withdrawals, retreats from the world. Our Lord has sent us out *into* the world to proclaim the Word of God, and the Word of God sheds light on our life. Our confidence, then, is in the Word of God alone, and in the Word of God not as conveying to us some supernatural truths about another and better world (though it does hold out before us the blessedness of complete redemption in the presence of God), but as casting light on the world and our life in it. The light it sheds is, moreover, an *indispensable* light for anyone who is trying to find the meaning of things (which is, after all, the real drive behind all genuine scientific work). The Law-word of God is universal, binding upon all and shedding its light for all, whether or not that Word is acknowledged. We are not to remain staring at the light – that would only cause blindness –, but to study the cosmos it illumines by the light it casts.

I say all this because it should be very clear that we are not proposing with our Institute just another Bible school or theological seminary. There are so many of these, and still Christians do not know their task in the world. Staring at the light does produce blindness, and we have lost generally, I think, the sense of the Scriptures for our lives even while we are richly equipped with Bible schools and seminaries. Further, it should be very clear that we are not interested at all in repristinating an older theism, philosophically reasoned in the Greek metaphysical way. We wish to have no traffic with any of those metaphysical arguments for a hidden realism of noumenal or supernatural 'entities' like 'God' and 'soul' which the eye of reason is supposedly able to discern behind the phenomena of the physical world. I refer to the sort of thing that we associate in our minds with the Scottish school, for instance, the kind of instruction that was long traditional in all American universities and colleges which regarded themselves in some sense as Christian. John Dewey was exposed to it at the outset of his academic career at the University of Vermont, but I myself was still taught such theism in my senior year at one of our American Christian colleges by the college president, who was a minister of the gospel. This was a very widespread custom. It was almost always the president who taught theism to the seniors, and the president was usually a clergyman. In the course of the second half of the nineteenth century John Dewey and a host of others like him rejected this whole way of establishing a world of substantial entities beyond the observable functional processes of this life. We are bound to say, on the point in question, that we find ourselves in complete agreement.

That does not mean that we do not have a controversy on with the men of our time. For the abandonment of metaphysically established substances does not mean, as so many 'moderns' have gratuitously assumed, that we are left with only an assortment of functional processes in this world which the several sciences are intended to explain. For, in the first place, it is the *unity* of things we experience when in life we turn our attention to rocks and trees and dogs and even other human beings. We experience each of these things as a unity, and not as an aggregate of a number of distinct functions. By its very (abstracting) nature, science cannot succeed in explaining this unity; yet our experience of the unity remains to be explained. Moreover, when we reflect scientifically on the several functional processes that occur in all created things, we discover that our experience is not just of a number of functions but of an *order* in the functions and of a functional *coherence*. Our scientific analysis, in other words, drives us beyond science to explain, as men, the unity of things to which the functional coherence points. Far from being a rehabilitation of the old metaphysics, this is simply a persistent effort to explain what in fact presents itself to us phenomenally in our experience. This state of affairs and this problem confronts every man.

Modern men who have committed themselves to science as the way to meaning are not able to find the meaning they are seeking. By employing scientific methods men can arrive at some understanding of the functional relations of things, but meaning is never a matter of scientific analysis. Meaning has to do with a religiously perceived unity in order and coherence. In the last analysis, man is a religious being, made to live in fellowship with God and in the experience of His favour. In such fellowship he is sensitive to truth and meaning. Having alienated himself from God, he can no longer experience the meaning of the creation.

This alienated man, then, is not, as he so often

thinks, just a scientist. He too is a believer, and he is that in virtue of God having created him that. That is what he remains, regardless of what in his lostness he says and thinks about himself. As a believer, he has tried in countless ways to construct some system of meaning for himself. One by one his creations have collapsed. At the moment of nihilism, the denial that there is any meaning, is widespread. Yet the nature of man asserts itself, and one can encounter the most pathetic longings. Witness the hippies of our continent, and the Maorist cult among European youth of the intellectual class. In his alienation from the God before Whom he might live, man is a believer, but he believes that other 'word' which, while living off the creative Word of God, suppresses and distorts it for its own rebellious purposes. Man is capable of strong delusion. For daily he is confronted with what God created, and its meaning. But he is in the grip of the great Rebel and Father of lies.

The cosmos of God is a theatre of contending spirits. Underlying everything else – in this age as in every, and in our individual lives as in the lives of institutions and whole societies – a great battle is being fought out. It is a battle of two spiritual powers. Once in our history, the two chief contenders in that battle met in a head-on encounter. Note particularly how that meeting broke up. The devil showed Jesus all the kingdoms of the world and the glory of them and said, "All these I will give you if you will fall down and worship me." Jesus' reply was immediate and short: "Begone, Satan! For it is written, 'You shall worship the Lord your God and him only shall you serve.'" Then, we read, the devil left him.

There are two spirits indeed. But only one is God. He has slain (and will slay) – we live between the times! – the other rebellious spirit by the breath of His Word. In the final analysis, the sovereignty of God in the cosmos is the source and ground of our confidence and our expectancy with respect to our Institute.

In the between-time, the battle, which is for nothing less than the entire creation and our whole lives, rages on from day to day. It is becoming more intense, more radical, and more sophisticated. It falls to us, Christians, to wage it continuously and resolutely, harmless as doves, but also wise or prudent as serpents. If we are to wage war prudently, the first requirement is that we understand the nature of the battle. In *this* battle, as to who has the authority to determine meaning, we have not begun to fight until we have learned not to rely on our metaphysical arguments and theological systems, and to place our confidence solely in the Word of God, which is powerful to open the heart, to beget to new life. It is a matter of bringing Spirit into play against spirit, ranging Word against word. We cannot play around with symptoms; we must get at the cause of the disease. The radical unbelief of our time can be effectively countered only when over against it there is placed a radical faith in the living, powerful and one Word of God. Over against the whispered suggestions of Satan must be set the Declaration or Statement of God. In this battle only the sovereign Word of God can win.

That we have come again to see the Word of God for what it is – this is the second and more immediate ground for our confidence and our expectancy with respect to what we are setting in motion today. Only when we have come to this insight does it become really possible for us in the great battle of spirits to counter point with point. Only now can we proceed with confidence in our chess game with Lenin's CHEKA.

The opening of this Institute is no luxury item; it is timely and it is urgent. As I said when I addressed the Fifteenth Anniversary Convention of the Christian Labour Association of Canada in April of this year:

> The most fundamental battle of our time is not to be thought of in the first place as one for the preservation of a familiar and so-called orthodox church organization, or of an abstract system of theological proposi-

tions. The struggle of our time goes much deeper: it is a struggle for the religious direction of human society in its totality. The battle of our time… is to determine which spirit is to give direction to our civilization. A church organization, or a world of Christian theological activity, standing alone within a culture all the other activities of which are directed by an anti-Christian spirit must remain impotent and has (by the very fact of its standing alone) already become irrelevant, and it will in the long run fade away. Even to preserve the organized church therefore, we must fight for an integral Christian society. Either there is a quickening of faith, which senses the religious unity of life, or there is the quiet accommodation, in almost imperceptible stages, to a way of life which does not, cannot, hear the Good Shepherd's voice. This is the quiet of the dead.

To that statement, I wish to add this: J. Gresham Machen, the founder of Westminster Theological Seminary, came in the course of his lifetime to the conviction that not a reductionist but an adequate statement of the Christian faith was the easiest to defend. If my own words arouse fear in you of the magnitude of the task, permit me to say that we will undoubtedly discover that an integral Christian life in the world is the easiest to accept and to defend. Everything depends upon the quickening of our heats to discern the spirits that are in the world. If there is no quickening, there is no defense either, of anything.

Here you have the phenomenon of 'rapidation': the whole world and all is inhabitants are now involved. Here is also intensification. And indeed, from the time of the French Revolution on, our days have been filled with mounting confusion on all sides, with revolutions and acts of violence which seem only to increase in tempo, in range and in intensity. Scientific research and technology, pursued by more and more people at more and more, and even larger, centres, constantly being stepped up more and more, are swept up onto this larger human platform. We see whole peoples, occupying large areas of the earth's surface, ravaged by unspeakable suffering. Think only of the emergence of national conscript armies (since Napoleon), of the shock created by the unrelenting trench warfare and by the poison gas of the First World War. Think of the Russian Revolution, the vast suffering it brought so sensitively described in Boris Pasternak's great novel, *Doctor Shivago*. Or turn your attention to the endless suffering of the dispersed Jews, and to its fiendish culmination in Hitler's "final solution" of that question. Here again we can gain some impression from Leon Wris' remarkable novel *Exodus*. And then there is China, Cuba, the continent of Africa, Latin America, the violence and the unrest in all our great urban centres. We have to call a halt; we cannot keep on thinking of it all.

And everywhere there is perplexity. Widespread collapse of faith in ancient certainties has led one Archbishop of Canterbury to speak of our time as one of "multiform bewilderment." Great masses of people today are aimless and lost: the nihilism which towards the middle of the nineteenth century took possession of the finer European spirits today has a hold of countless thousands. There is the phenomenon of the hippie cult, and of the New Left. Through everything there is a determined, radical carrying through of the secularization of our lives. A stark this-world-only mentality is suddenly bursting out all over, having quietly penetrated to all circles and levels of our western society, and to every nook and cranny of the world of theory. The apparent irresistibility of its advance is sapping the strength of many Christians, leaving them stunned and nerveless.

Our Lord told us (Luke 21) that when these things begin to happen, far from becoming stunned and nerveless, we are to look up and lift up our heads because our redemption is drawing nigh. I take that to mean that we are to be inspired with courage and faith in the knowledge that the Lord is at hand, and also our own full bodily redemption. In other words, that we are to be not faint but believing. But faith in the Scriptures commits the believer to acts of faith that relate to his time and situation. Now there may well come a time when human society is so completely under the control of the Evil One that Christians will not have the freedom to act. At this very moment, while I am speaking to you, Christians are severely restricted in this very regard in large areas of the world. The Christian, no matter what his circumstances, will always be able to look up and lift up his head. He can do that on the rack or as the flames begin to rise all around him; before the guillotine or in the torture chamber of Lublanka prison. If that is all his society will permit him to do, then that will be the way in which he should express his courage and faith. But today we are thankful that it is still possible for us, here and now, to take concerted historical action. We are grateful that there is yet time to act in a decisive way towards confronting the dominant spirit of our time in a head-on encounter. We are particularly grateful that it is possible for us to do this by opening this Institute, for in this way we are doing it in a fashion expertly tailored to the peculiar conditions of our historical situation.

God has made it possible for us to open our Institute. He has done it in a way that only God can do. But men too are necessary to do those things which it is up to men to do. And so, in the second place this morning, I should say, I think, a very brief word about a very human, down-to-earth feeling we all have of great relief that all the uncertainties, the struggles, and the hard work which had to be lived through in order to make this day possible are now behind us. It is already beginning to be difficult to imagine those earliest years of our Association's history when our strong conviction about what had to be done was just about all we had, and thus stood out in its beautiful religious simplicity. There followed stormy years of articulating that conviction, of relating it to our human and material resources and to the surrounding Canadian social and academic situation. It is good that at first we were not able to foresee the tortuous path we would have to pursue. But we did formulate an Educational Creed, and succeeded in giving it a status in our society. Over the years we succeeded in interesting a significant number of our students and young teachers for a higher education that is given its direction by the Word of God. Then only two years ago, after many years of quiet but steady planning, in a widely circulated report entitled *Place and Task of an Institute of Reformed Scientific Studies*, we proposed to Christian people the establishment of an Institute, to be situated here in the city of Toronto, as the first step in our controlled and orderly advance towards a Free Reformed University on the North American continent.

Especially since that time the people have rallied to our call in ever-increasing numbers. Very recently, the circle of interest has widened appreciably. Particularly striking and heart-warming has been the whole-hearted support we have received, in both East and West, from so many of that younger generation of students and teachers. And now today we are here to dedicate and to open that Institute. This is the very first time that all of us – members, Board, staff, students, guests and that very much esteemed wider circle of interested persons – are gathered together in one place. It is, I believe, the first time that any of us in the Association for Reformed Scientific Studies, in over ten years of work together – and they have been ten exacting years – have officially paused in our work. This is the first occasion on which we take time out to savour the delights of partial fulfillment and of the unusually rich blessing which the Lord of Good has showered down upon us here in this Canadian land in our collective life as an Association.

It is a good thing that we do this. The life of men restored to fellowship with God is a collective life, and it is a life of joy and gladness. We have reached today the culmination of the first important stage of our work.

We found and were able to purchase a fitting home for our Institute in the desired section of Toronto. We have secured just the kind of teaching fellow that we had hoped for, and we all know by now how hard Dr. Hart can work and how devoted he is to this work. Through someone's anonymous, but very thoughtful, generosity we are privileged to have with us for these momentous days the man who was in fact the first to be appointed to the staff of our Institute, though now for a number of reasons he will actually be the second to assume his task, viz. an appointment in the field of law and political science. I refer to Mr. Barnard Zylstra, who together with his wife has come from Amsterdam, the Netherlands, to celebrate with us here. Although not personally known until this week to a great many of us, the Zylstras really belong to the official family, and as in any family it would have been a less joyous experience today if they had not been here. And now the work of our Institute is about to begin. I think that all we lack at this moment is the toast, but we had better reserve that for the dinner this afternoon, hoping that it will not get too black from its long wait in the toaster. Today, friends, we experience covenant joys. We thank God, and take courage.

In the third place we experience this morning a feeling of intense expectancy. You will have sensed it when I spoke of this day as a decisive turning point, crucial for all English-speaking nations. You will have detected it when I referred to a re-alignment of forces that has been taking place with the avowed purpose of bringing home to the hearts and minds of this student generation, in a way surpassing any hitherto attempted, the claim which the revelation of God in Jesus Christ makes upon the entire scientific and scholarly enterprise of man. You will recall that I spoke of what we purpose to do in our Institute as a radical Christian proposal for radical times. In that connection I referred to Karl Marx's well-known statement that to be radical is to get to the root of the question.

Our Institute is indeed being welcomed with an intense expectancy. There is quite generally among us the feeling that we are beginning something that is new, different, and very important to the well-being of the Christian cause. There is the feeling that this Institute is going to help in a very direct way to meet a pressing and fundamental need of our time, a need which has long waited to be satisfied and which, for whatever reasons, is simply not being met by Christians elsewhere. The expectancy among us is almost palpable, and it appears to be born of a certain confidence. What is it that gives rise to this feeling of newness? What is the ground of our confidence and our expectancy?

At this point my mind goes back to a stunning moment in Leon Uris' novel of a few years back entitled *Exodus*. I have no doubt that many of you will be able to recall the incident with me. Don Landan, age fifteen, one of the few Polish Jews who had survived the hell of the Warsaw ghetto uprising of 1939, and that still more evil thing, the Anschwiz-Birkenaw extermination camp, is at last on his way to Palestine in company with other Auschwitz refugees. After spending the winter months in Vienna recuperating, these hapless survivors embark in the springtime on another train that carries them through the Brenner Pass into Italy. The train stops near Lake Como outside Milan. Here, at an isolated siding, they encounter for the first-time men in fighting uniforms and wearing a Star of David on their arms. These soldiers were in fact units of the Palestine Brigade of the British Army stationed in Italy as occupation forces. But for all practical purposes, they were under the command of Aliyah Bet and Palmach, agents from Palestine who had integrated with these units. At the sight of these young fighting men, the camp survivors are stunned. In Mr. Uris' own words, they

> could not comprehend men in fighting uniforms wearing a Star of David on their arm. The Star of David had always been the insignia of the ghetto. No Jews, except in the ghetto uprisings, had fought under a Star of

David for nearly two thousand years. The soldiers were kind and some spoke Yiddish and all spoke Hebrew and they were gentle but they seemed to be a different breed of Jew.[1]

That, I submit, is a fascinating episode. I find myself returning to it again and again. What makes it so fascinating is the question which, just beneath the surface of the daily round of experience, is uppermost in every Jewish mind and which since the Second World War presses with more poignancy and a greater urgency than ever before for solution. Why the Jew? What does it mean, in the last analysis, to be a Jew? In the nineteenth and early twentieth centuries many Jews of central Europe had done their best to throw off their distinctiveness and had cast themselves fully as enlightened moderns into the general social and cultural life of Europe. Many of these had married into non-Jewish families. In the end, however, it was all to no avail: they were marked as Jews, there remained something Jewish about them, and in time of great persecution many of these Jews once again allied themselves with the lot of the Jewish people. What is it to be a Jew? Is it something ethnic, or cultural, or is it a matter of religion? Deep-probing articles on the subject are being written

---

1. See Leon Uris, *Exodus* (New York, NY.: Bantam, 1983).

today, but no answer seems to be found.

The question remains unanswered because the Jew no longer lives before God by the light of His Word. The Jews have always been the people of the Law, but they have long since lost any real insight into what the Law is. God's Law is God's Word. Because God is God, His every Word is Law. From the very first words of the Bible we hear, "And God said, Let there be" this and that. All such creative words are the Law. The Law is what causes creatures and the whole creation to hang together; it determines the conditions of all creaturely existence. It itself is *centrated* in the religious law of life: Walk before me according to my commandments and live. Here we have the heart of the creation. The Law determines what it means to *live* before God, or to *die* before God. The Jews were the people of God's choice. He made Himself known to them; to them He gave Himself. They were His people and He was their God. He was with them and for them. The Law simply gives expression to this covenantal fellowship. It is the Word of the living God by which the men of His choice live before His face, by which they are enabled, in their manifold inter-creaturely relationships, to bring all the potentialities and capacities which God Himself has laid in human existence, both individual and collective, to the fullest and richest possible realization in a service of God. This is the true Kingdom of God and here is the true *joie de vivre* which makes one to dance before Jehovah.

But this central, full religious sense of the Law of God the Jew had lost, and in its place had come an abstract formalism, a precisionism, a narrow preoccupation with the many words and prescriptions in the Law. The Chasidim, i.e. the devout ones, withdrew from the normal 'round' of life activities to make meditation on the words of the Law, the centre of their thought and practical life. They developed a religion of ritual piety for their individual personal conduct, and this led to casuistry, to moralism, to legalism. There were those who passed their days in detailed eisegesis of the many scriptural injunctions. A theologically qualified scientism grew up: one had to learn by painful study how to be "righteous" and the more deeply a religious man penetrated into the secrets of Talmudic casuistry, the higher his religious perfection mounted. Religion became a matter of the trained intellect. There were also the Kabbalist, who sought in the words of the Law for hidden, esoteric meanings based on mysticism and numerology. For centuries, Judaism had been a subjectivistic, introverted sort of thing. It is no wonder that to the miserable survivors of ghetto and camp for whom Judaism had meant such things, those enterprising, confident young soldiers living an active life of service in the world in connection with the re-birth of a Jewish state appeared as a different breed of Jew.

I certainly would not wish to appear to be equating the political activisms of the emerging Israeli with what the Scripture knows as living before the face of the God of the covenant. After Jesus, who was born in Bethlehem of David's line, at a moment of historic decision was rejected as the Anointed or Messiah who was to redeem Israel, it became impossible for the Jew, as long as he persevered in this rejection, to understand the Law of God. Or, to use Paul's momentous language in Romans 11, an insensibility has come upon part of Israel until the full number of the Gentiles come in. The youthful representatives of modern Israel may feel an aversion to the various escape-mechanisms by which the Jews, through their long introverted history, have avoided the world and society; they may experience estrangement from the habitual Jewish retreats, from a full-orbed life in the world. No more than the others do they possess any real insight into what it is to be a Jew and to have the Law. Yet somehow, we feel a measure of sympathy for their aversions and their estrangements. For somewhere in their beings they sense that whatever it is to be a Jew, it must have to do with life, with fullness of life, with life in the world. Somewhere within them they have felt, and felt strongly, that the Law of life cannot be what the Talmudic scholars, the Chasidim, and the Kabbalists have made of it.

Point Counter Point

In the great Archetypal Encounter between Christ and Satan, each spirit has spoken his 'word'. Satan as well as Christ made use of the written scriptures. But each time Christ has checkmated Satan. For although with Satan there is always the pretense of living by the Word of God, actually this rebellious creature had wrenched words loose from their sense in the one Word and – biblicistically – produced many separate pseudo-'words'. Jesus' replies return us to the very religious-covenantal centre of the divine Word. Satan speaks his 'word'; it is as if we hear Jesus say: Check. Again Satan has a 'word' ready, and again from Jesus we hear: Check. This is the real Checkmate of history. The 'word' of the One is the Word of (a) God. "One little word shall fell him," we sing in Martin Luther's great Reformation hymn. This is our confidence that the Word of God has prevailed and will continue to prevail.

Nevertheless, in the continuing historical struggle of human spirits, in the multitudinous chess games that are being played by human agents, each of those central 'words' – the pseudo-'word' of Satan or Christ's Word of God – is in need of articulation in connection with the social, the economic, the political, generally, the cultural conditions of our bodily existence. To us, men, belongs the responsibility for relating the central 'word' to the conditions of our life in the world. And right here we Christians are at a decided disadvantage today, and our Institute is a desperate need.

In order to make very clear what I have in mind, let me remind you of two important anniversaries that will soon be widely celebrated. There is, first, the 50th anniversary of the great Russian Revolution, the so-called October Revolution or *coup d'état* of the Bolsheviks, which occurred on October 25 (November 7 of our calendar), 1917. Second, on October 31 we mark the 450th anniversary of Martin Luther's affixing a series of theses to the door of the castle church in Wittenberg.

The events these anniversaries will commemorate and the movements they call to mind represent a big part of the spiritual pilgrimage of modern western man. We ought not to think of the Russian Revolution of 1917, for instance, as an isolated event in European history. It is but one of the most recent links, along with the communist revolution of Chairman Mao's China, in a chain of revolutions which has made the past 200 years an Age of Revolution, and for which we can take the French Revolution as a convenient starting-point. The historical connections are clear. Mao, for example, when he was a young man, read assiduously a Chinese magazine which brought translations of Voltaire, Diderot, and in general of the French thinkers who had contributed to the coming of the French Revolution. Even the French Revolution is only the breaking out into overt deeds of a way of thinking which dates from modern man's liberation of himself from the medieval church and from all outside influence, including, indeed especially, God. Autonomy or freedom, understood as freedom from any influence coming from outside the human subject, was the central idea of the Renaissance. Man was cock o' the walk, and his goal, self-established dominion or rule over nature. Rejection, overturning of the divinely established Order of Creation, this is the hallmark of modern humanism. When man lives out of such a spirit of rebellion, we have, as Groen van Prinsterer called it, the 'permanent Revolution'.

For a time the coming of the Reformation – and even the Counter-reformation in the Roman Catholic Church – succeeded in stemming this tide of humanism, at least in great areas of Europe. Over against the radical this worldliness of the Renaissance and of that type of Humanism which oriented itself to the ancient Greek or Roman writers, the early work of both Luther and Calvin put man radically before God and His

Word. But when the Reformation movement had been diverted from its original goals, and after the Wars of Religion had used up the religious élan released by the original Reformation impulses, and also brought widespread disillusionment with the Christian churches, a revival of humanism, strengthened now by its alliance with the development of modern science, arose. The Enlightenment was a shriller, tenser version of the same humanism as that of the Renaissance. It also reached more people, and penetrated into more areas of their lives.

Once again, the Evangelical Revival and the Great Awakening of the 18th century offered resistance to the spread of unbelief, but this time there was not the depth of insight that the Reformers Luther and Calvin had possessed, so that the fundamental and radical opposition of Christianity to humanism was not seen, or put, so clearly as these men had done. Jonathan Edwards is an excellent example of how such a mind, increasingly caught up in the ways of thinking of the 'modern mind', finds itself thwarted in stating the Christian 'word' as it must be stated. In the later men there is more of a grasping at immediate solutions, and it is chiefly the individual soul that is to be saved. Failing to confront humanism in any central and comprehensive way, the Evangelical Revival stemmed the revolutionary tide less than the Reformation had done, and in fewer places. The western world was rapidly becoming post-Christianly pagan. By the middle of the nineteenth century the educated class of Europe had broken overwhelmingly with any Christian point of view.

In this way we can understand that humanism has been the dominant cultural driving force or 'mind' in modern western civilization, which, by taking possession of the hearts of untold millions, and by gaining control of our centres of authority and of education, has undergone development and been given expression in and through the successive experiences of western men.

> It is interesting to observe that the phenomenon we know generally as "the Christian college" dates from this period, or later, and *far from having in view any reformation of the sciences and of scholarship,* seemed to see itself chiefly as the guardian of some denomination's or of fundamentalism's youth by holding them together and aloof from the penetrating secularism, the evolutionism and the higher criticism of the age.

In this dominant humanistic camp there has been a continual drift to the Left. For while it was the Moderates or Liberals to whom the direction of affairs fell after the first stage of the (French) Revolution had runs its course, it had been the Radicals, or confident believers in the powers of man's autonomous Reason to create a heavenly city right here on earth, who had set the course of events in the first place. The Moderates had not some other goal or direction to put over against that of those they have taught us to call the Extremists; they moved generally forward in the same revolutionary stream, but their adjustments out of so-called practical and utilitarian considerations made them appear more neutral and tended to obscure the driving religions principle that was yet operative in the course of events. There is nothing mysterious, really, about the continual tendency in modern society to the Left.

During the 19th century, radicalism still remained a peripheral movement, but the scope of influence of the revolutionary ideas was considerably enlarged. After the French Revolution, the struggle between the classes began anew in Switzerland, which was now so stimulated by the French example that the object was no longer merely to regain ancient popular rights, but to introduce the new abstract 'equality' and 'fraternity'. The year 1798 even saw the complete overthrow of the Swiss constitution and the establishment of the Helvetic Republic. With the subsequent revolutions of 1830 and 1848, the spirit of humanism, in its radical form, was brought down to the great masses of workers, who, as a result of the Industrial Revolution and its injustices, were becoming estranged from the Christian Church even while they were beginning to find their collective voice. The year 1848 is also the year of the publication of the *Communist Manifesto* of Marx and Engels.

While the spirit of humanism was thus gaining adherents and taking on more and more articulate form, the representatives of the Reformation became diverted from the central religious conflict as posed by Luther and Calvin and, in answering the subtle attacks of the skilled Catholic theologians, spent their energies in mastering the details of Aristotelian metaphysics for theological dialectic. Protestants came to withdraw either into a very restricted world of theological argument and investigation or, pietistically, into their private personal lives of 'devotion', failing to understand that the Word of God was given as light under which man was to live his life by on this earth. Many Protestants, having first accepted a scholastic division into 'natural' and 'spiritual', proceeded to allow the humanistic spirit which had given form to what they thought of as their 'natural' life, to engulf them entirely. By stages they had become essentially humanist thinkers. This explains many of the woes of the present theological world and of Protestants generally. In none of the Protestant groups was the central "word" of Christ taking on flesh and blood as it was being related to the conditions of our creaturely existence in the continuing experiences of men through the modern centuries.

Only since the last decades of the previous century do we see a fundamental crisis of modern western culture arising: the skilled observer can detect (1) a crisis in foundations of the long-dominant humanistic movement; (2) the re-birth of scholastic (particularly of Thomistic) philosophy, especially since the encyclical *Aeberni Patris* of 1879 of the great Pope Leo *XIII*; and (3) the rise of a more radically scriptural way of life and thought, with a corresponding independent philosophical reflection, in the Protestant circles which have remained true to the foundations of the Reformation, and which profited from the culture-historical investigations of Abraham Kuyper in the Netherlands and from work done at the Free Reformed University of Amsterdam which he and others founded in 1880.

Herewith a momentous transition-period in world history has announced itself, in which a struggle, as yet undetermined, for the spiritual control of our western culture is being carried on. In the Catholic church, a battle has more recently begun to rage about the status of the scholastic way of thinking. In Protestant circles, almost exclusively at the Free University, or at a few centres influenced by this university, has significant cultural work been done by the light of the Word of God, and even then it has been precious little, significant though that little may be.

Thus we are faced with this appalling situation: that in a world where the representatives and spokesmen of humanism, the dominant cultural movement of the modern centuries, keenly and radically aware of the status of their position as never before, have very widely experienced a collapse of faith in their position, the adherents of the Way of Christ lack generally any articulation of that 'word' of Christ relevant to the cultural and historical experience of modern men which might induce them to listen to that word. The 'word' of Christ, which felled the Deceiver of men once and can overcome Satan's hold on the hearts of individual men, has not taken on body in terms of the conditions of human life, and thus I, not at once, have seen as having anything to do with our living in the world.

This is what Harry Blamires meant in the significant first part of his widely overlooked volume *The Christian Mind*. If we use the word 'mind' to mean a collectively accepted set of notions and attitudes, we can speak, he argues, of 'the modern mind' but not of a Christian mind. And by that he means to say that "in contradistinction to the secular mind, no vital Christian mind plays fruitfully, as a coherent and recognizable influence, upon our social, political or cultural life."

He points to recent criticism of the values of our culture, made from a humanistic standpoint. These critics, he writes, and I am going to quote him at some length:

> are all contributing to a living dialogue. This dialogue is being carried on in our midst, a feature of our intellectual life. It presses immediately upon us. It threads its way through our lives if our lot is cast among men of intelligence. It is intertwined with our friendships and meets us in quiet reflective moments as we take up a book in the bookshop or the library, or pick up a week-end journal in the home. The stream of talk among thinking people today presupposes a knowledge of the rigorous critique to which humanism is subjecting contemporary civilization. For the books I have [in mind] show the modern mind at work on its prophetic side. They are born of the secular mind and in turn they nourish the secular mind. They sell in thousands because they fall naturally and easily, upon publication, into a living field of discourse… The thinking Christian has to step in and out of the field of discourse in which current values are thus analyzed, like a man putting on and off protective clothing. Joining, as a reader on a conversationalist, in the discussion of the issues raised, one has to become

temporarily – mentally – a non-Christian. Otherwise one carries on a private monologue. This is because, on entering the field of discourse, one finds one is the only Christian present... What, then, is the position of the thinking Christian, face to face with the cultural situation which I have described? As he reads the things worth reading, he is continually meeting with accounts of the human situation or with critical analyses of man's current lot, which make him sit up and say: This is profound and penetrating. This represents a deep and wholly human response to present-day life. It is crucial, fundamental, and illuminating that it cannot be overlooked. It touches me pre-eminently *as a Christian*. Yet this writer is not a Christian. I share his vision for a moment over this issue or that, and the next minute I am jerked back into awareness that he and I are poles apart, separated by a chasm, by a contradiction in our most basic presuppositions. But (and this is the tragedy) the only way I can pursue this vital current of thought further is by more reading of non-Christian literature written by skeptics, and by discussion of it *within the intellectual frame of reference* which these skeptics have manufactured. In short, there is no current Christian dialogue on this topic. There is no Christian conversation which I can enter, bringing this topic or this vision with me... We twentieth-century Christians have chosen the way of compromise. We withdraw our Christian consciousness from the fields of public, commercial and social life. When we enter these fields we are compelled to accept for purposes of discussion the secular frame of reference established there. We have to use the only language spoken in these areas. Our own Christian language is no longer understood there. Moreover, we ourselves have so long ceased to use it except for discussion of the moral, the liturgical… that it is rusty and out of date. We have no Christian vocabulary to match the complexities of contemporary political, social and industrial life. How should we have? A language is nurtured on usage, not on silence, however high-principled. And we have long since ceased to bring Christian judgment to bear upon the secular public world… The Church's virtual withdrawal from these fields has left the pragmatists and utilitarians in power. It has led to the decay of the Christian mind. And now, by reaction, it has begotten a brood of frustrated Christians who try to cultivate their own souls but, outside of that, just don't know what to do.

So Blamires.

In the world of science and scholarship the situation is no different. The humanist spirit has prevailed there too, and Christians have been conspicuous either by their absence or by their silence and accommodation.

There has been, for example, no general re-structuring of bodies of concepts and terms that stems from an original religious understanding of the claim the Word of God makes upon such work. And certainly there has been no historical process of development of such a re-structuring that would furnish a tool for thought adequate to deal with the accumulation of human experience in the modern centuries (which *has* been given interpretation by the humanist mind).

It is to relate the 'word' of Christ to the conditions of our life and the concerns of our time, and to do that without imbibing the spirit of our time, that we have set ourselves to erect this Institute. The rapid development of our Institute now lies urgently upon us. Our times increasingly demand longer and higher education; more and more of our sons and daughters are going to have to become involved in the life of the world of science and scholarship, with its peculiar problems. In the past, generation upon generation, much of the best talent God has given us in our families, in our sons and daughters has been weaned from us by humanistic agencies of higher education. Often we have not understood as parents what has been happening to our more gifted children. Perhaps our children themselves did not understand. But what agony of spirit there has been in the family circle! Yet we went on, breeding other children, providing material (which God had entrusted to us) for humanism's form-giving. No longer can we stand idly by in this – both for ourselves and our society – so fateful Contest of the spirits. We must now concentrate on the task we collectively assume; we must rapidly develop our capabilities.

The introduction of our Institute into the life of our North American continent is not to be construed as one more instance of Christians' following, in spite of all the fine language, the way of cultural withdrawal. The 'word' of Christ is a word to all men. But in order for that 'word' to be presented effectively to the world, Christians must have a home base where they can strengthen and develop their resources. Such 'withdrawal' in order to 'return' is a necessary condition for any dialogue, whether it be a debate, a game, or military strategy. This is not the same as cultural withdrawal.

In all antithetical activity there is the element of hostility. In Hegelian or analytical dialectic, the opposition is overcome in a higher synthesis. That is not true of the religious antithesis that has concerned us here this morning. There will be no reconciliation of the opposed 'words', and the need for 'withdrawal' in order to 'return' is indeed evidence that the source of the opposition lies deeper than Hegel or Marx suspected. The Word of God is to fell the enemy. And this God

Himself did, at the Temptation, and will yet finally do at the second Coming of our Lord Jesus Christ.

But the Word of God is also for the salvation of men and for the heading of the nations. The 'word' must be kept pure, for by His Word God reconciles men to Himself, and He has committed unto us the ministry of reconciliation. We remember that we are men, ourselves rebels against the most high God, who have been made recipients of His grace. Our erection of this Institute must be seen as a development of our work of reconciliation. Here again the Word of God will prevail; it will accomplish what it was given to do.

Closing Words

As we approach the moment of the official opening of the Institute, we recall once more that our confidence for all that it is intended to do – is in the Word of God alone. The God who came near in Jesus Christ is our strength; His Word is our life. Mindful of what we have said of our calling to be agents of reconciliation, our hearts cry out in the words of an Old Testament prophet: *O earth, earth, earth, hear the Word of God and live*. Let us therefore, for ourselves, this morning declare, publicly and communally, that our help always and only, also in the erection of an Institute for the advancement of Christian scholarship, is in the Name of the Lord, who made the heavens and the earth; Who is, as His parting word to us in the last book of the Bible says, root and offspring of David, the bright morning star, that is to say, the One who though of the line of David was also his Lord – Ruler thus over all things and all history in the majesty of sovereignty, and at the same time the Saviour, the Promise of a new day, of complete (cosmic) redemption and final glory. The Alpha and Omega, Who is and Who was and Who is to come, the Almighty. This God, ladies and gentlemen, the Creator of heaven and earth, is our God in Christ. He is the Sovereign of the universe, but He is not a God far off. For He is also David's offspring, Immanuel, God-with-us-men. He is our hope and joy forever.

With our hearts extended to Him, beseeching Him to establish this day's work of our hands, we proceed now to the Act of Dedication.

ABOUT THE AUTHOR

Howard Evan Runner (1916-2002) graduated with honours from Wheaton College. He earned a Bachelor's degree in theology from Westminster Theological Seminary. He subsequently received an appointment as a junior fellow at Harvard University. After earning a Master's degree in theology at Westminster he traveled to The Free University of Amsterdam where he earned his Ph.D. degree. Runner taught Philosophy at Calvin College from 1951 until his retirement in 1981. He is the author of *The Christian and the World*, *The Relation of the Bible to Learning*, and several other publications collected in the *Walking in the Way of the Word: The Collected Writings of H. Evan Runner*.

PAIDEIA MONOGRAPHS

Other Titles (2020–):

The Development of Calvinism in North America
H. Evan Runner

The Radical Christian Facing Today's Political Malaise
H. Evan Runner

Christ and Christianity
Herman Bavinck

The Analogical Concepts
Herman Dooyeweerd

The Concept of Sovereignty in Modern Jurisprudence and Political Science
Herman Dooyeweerd

The Criteria of Progressive and Reactionary Tendencies in History
Herman Dooyeweerd

The Secularization of Science
Herman Dooyeweerd

Looking for more?
Visit www.paideiapress.ca

www.ingramcontent.com/pod-product-compliance
Lightning Source LLC
Chambersburg PA
CBHW051958290426
44110CB00015B/2300